Otto Piddle would have been a sure bet to win this year's Chump's Landing Overland Obstacle Bicycle Race, if only his daring bicycle stunt hadn't landed him in a heap. And now it looks as though Montana Muldoon—that muscle-bounder from Setonville—will be the winner, unless Chump's Landing can produce another cyclist to take Otto Piddle's place.

Hub is bound and determined that someone from Chump's Landing *will* win the race. And with help from his best friend, Spooner, Hub tries a few tricks to keep the trophy where it rightfully belongs. After all, it *is* an obstacle race, so what's the harm of adding extra obstacles?

With a cast of colorful new characters, including a pair of pals, their sporting teacher, a town beauty, two feuding doctors, and even a gaggle of geese, Robert Newton Peck has spun another funny tale around the lives and times in a small town.

Books by Robert Newton Peck

A Day No Pigs Would Die
Path of Hunters
Millie's Boy
Soup
Fawn
Wild Cat
Bee Tree (*poems*)
Soup and Me
Hamilton
Hang for Treason
Rabbits and Redcoats
King of Kazoo (*a musical*)
Trig
Last Sunday
The King's Iron
Patooie
Soup for President
Eagle Fur
Trig Sees Red
Basket Case
Mr. Little
Hub

ROBERT NEWTON PECK

HUB

ILLUSTRATED BY TED LEWIN

Alfred A. Knopf · New York

This is a Borzoi Book published by Alfred A. Knopf, Inc.

Library of Congress Cataloging in Publication Data. Peck, Robert Newton. Hub. Summary: When their teacher enters the annual Chump's Landing Overland Obstacle Bicycle Race, Horrace Hubert and his best friend Spooner Jitwell do everything they can to make sure she wins the silver trophy. [1. Bicycle racing—Fiction] I. Title. PZ7.P339Hu 1979 Fic] 78-11763 ISBN 0-394-83968-4 ISBN 0-394-93968-9 lib. bdg.

HUB

"Here he comes, Hub," said Spooner.

"Yup," I said, "wagon and all."

Spooner Jitwell was pointing up Main Street, while all eyes in town were fixed on the team of bay horses, with Otto Piddle holding the reins. As it was Saturday afternoon, plenty of folks had come to town in order to witness the impossible.

Spooner asked, "Think he'll really do it, Hub?"

"Well," I said, raking a sleeve across my face to blot my nostrils, "I heard Otto claim he can do it."

"Ya know, Hub," snorted Spooner, "I don't guess *anybody* could jump a bicycle up in the air and over a team of horses."

From the driver's bench of his wagon, Mr. Piddle was waving to folks on both sides of Main Street, and once in a while he'd tip his cap to a lady or two. Otto Piddle sure knew how to put on a show. Not one soul in the town of Chump's Landing wanted to miss what was about to happen.

"Otto's painted up his wagon," said Spooner.

"He sure has," I said. "Real fresh."

The wagon itself looked sort of like a big sandwich standing on its edges instead of lying flat on a plate. Each flank of the wagon sported a big square sign, in red, white, and blue, which clearly read PIDDLE'S PEDALS, a real holler of an advertisement for Otto's bicycle shop. Bicycles were the chief subject of conversation in Chump's Landing, thanks to the efforts of Otto Piddle, who owned a thriving business.

The big signs fluttered in the April breeze, causing the letters of PIDDLE'S PEDALS to wave proudly. It looked to me as though Otto had painted the signs on a pair of old white bedsheets, tacked on to a pair of large wooden frames.

"Where's his bicycle?" asked Spooner.

"In his wagon, most likely. Between the signs."

Mr. Piddle commanded a "Whoa," and the team snorted to a stop, first making a quarter of a turn so that the horses faced Rickert's Grocery, with their rumps aimed across the street at Quimby's Drygoods Store. At the moment, the stores weren't rushing much of a business. I saw Mr. Rickert standing in his white apron outside of his grocery. Behind his ear rested the yellow stub of a pencil.

Reaching under the seat of his wagon, Otto produced a U.S. Army bugle, which he put to his talented lips in order to blow "First Call." Everybody clapped.

"Chump's Landing sure is a lucky town," I said, "to have a bicycle champ like Otto Piddle."

Spooner agreed. "We certain are."

"I'd like to be a champeen someday," I said, "soon as I grow up."

"You?"

"Sure. It would feel real nifty to be known as Horrace Hubert, the champ of the whole wide world."

"Champ at what?"

"Well," I said with a hopeful shrug, "I don't guess I've quite figured that part out yet."

"Let me know," said Spooner, "soon as you do, Hub."

"You'll be the first."

"I better be." Spooner Jitwell doubled up his big fat fist to cuddle his knuckles under my skinny chin. Just the thought of Spooner's fist could darn near make my nose bleed. He was half a year older than I was, but weighed half a sack more, and he could gnaw the cap off a bottle of Dr. Sippy's Sodapop Tonic with his bare teeth. Not only that. I once saw him take a bite out of a Harry Lauder phonograph record and then chew up the pieces until they were little black triangles.

"What's he doing, Hub?"

"He's lifting out his bicycle," I said.

Several pairs of willing Chump's Landing hands rushed to help Otto Piddle unload his bike from the open tailgate at the rear of the wagon. A hushed "Ah" oozed from the crowd, for Otto's famous yellow bicycle was doggone close to being a town landmark. In shape it was like any other bicycle; a tiny dragwheel in back, with a giant pedalwheel up front that stood taller than the brim of Otto's cap.

Mr. Piddle had red hair, a red mustache, plus the face and form of a born champion. For the past two years, he had won the big silver trophy, awarded to the winner

of the Chump's Landing Overland Obstacle Bicycle Race.

"Boy oh boy," said Spooner, "I'd swap half the cows in Pa's barn just to be Otto Piddle for one day."

"Yeah," I said, "like today."

Hearing a sigh, I turned to squint over my left shoulder to catch a glimpse of Miss Sashay Freshmeadow, who, according to most of the local citizenry, was far and away the prettiest gal in Chump's Landing. Even though she

was a bit on the chubby side. I looked at her while she looked at Otto Piddle as though he was spice. Lace glove and all, her hand went up to her throat as if to admit that just beholding Mr. Otto Piddle sent vapors down her gullet.

"There's the mayor," said Spooner.

Sure enough, we saw E. Clarence Smather, all gussied up in his church suit, and it wasn't even Sunday until tomorrow. He was smiling, an act which hardly made news, as he even smiled for five whole minutes the day he got kicked unconscious by Hoover Glint's horse, Albert.

"And now," said Mayor Smather, "we shall all witness a spectacle of derring-do never before seen here in Chump's Landing. But first I shall call on Reverend Roop to lead us all in a moment of——"

We all bowed our heads.

"Mayor . . ."

"Yes?"

"Reverend Roop left."

"Uh, in that case," stuttered Mayor Smather, "we can perhaps dispense with a——"

We unbowed our heads.

"Hey," said Spooner, "get a load of all them planks."

Those planks, I silently corrected him. That was a habit that I had ceased to practice aloud, mainly due to the fact that Spooner Jitwell's kidney punch could be far more convincing than my grammar.

"They're setting something up, Hub."

"Sure enough are."

"Ya think it's the runway?"

I nodded. Half a dozen fellows erected a ramp of boards, a slanted incline that led from the ground to near a height of six feet.

"Hub, you reckon that's for his takeoff?"

"Yup," I said.

"I can't believe he'll do it," said Spooner.

"Why not?"

"Well, because to see somebody bicycle fast enough to jump it over a team of horses isn't a sight ya see every day."

"Nope," I told Spooner, "I don't guess it is."

"I wonder why Otto wants to do it."

"My father says that it's good for his business. I suppose a stunt like this takes a famous fellow like Mr. Otto Piddle and helps freshen his fame."

"Ya think so?"

"Either that or he wants to get the attention of Miss Sashay Freshmeadow."

Spooner shot a glance over my shoulder. "She sure watches Otto like he was gumdrops."

I agreed. I still thought she was chubby. A bit like Spooner in that respect.

"Hub, I bet Amoeba May Kiliper looks at you the way Miss Freshmeadow makes eyes at Otto."

"Who cares about Amoeba May Kiliper?" I said, trying to make my voice sound as if Spooner was talking about a catfish. But my throat fluttered. And my heart sort of did likewise, because if there was one girl at school that could clogdance my tonsils, it was Amoeba May Kiliper.

The planks were in place.

Mr. Otto Piddle got a heft up onto the high seat of his bicycle, his gifted feet astride the pedals that sprouted from the center of the big yellow circle that was its front wheel. Inside his bright green knickers, the knees of Otto Piddle churned up and down as he rode his bicycle around in figure eights. Dust kicked up from the little tire that trailed behind the big one. Back he went, in a serpent of curves from one boardwalk of Main Street to the other across the tan dirt street. No one single wagon or buckboard dared to budge as Otto measured the distance to the ramp of planks with his practiced eye.

Mr. Philo McMurtree quickly filled the rut of his big camera flasher, ready to capture an historical photo for the front page of this coming week's *Chump's Landing Trumpet*. His assistant of the moment was Goose Gifford, who nervously fingered the trigger cord. I watched Goose's foot accidentally kick over the jar of flash powder, thinking to myself that I sure wouldn't let old Goose take charge of a jellybean.

"Doggone it, Goose," said a frowning Mr. McMurtree, "that there flash powder cost me six bits a jar."

"Watch the birdie," said Goose.

"Not yet," said Mr. McMurtree. "Otto's all the way down the street." Our town photographer then ducked under the black shroud of his camera, bobbing his head around like a melon in bed.

"Here comes Otto!"

All necks strained to the left on our side of the street. Nobody even breathed.

"Now?" asked Goose.

"No," said Mr. McMurtree, "not now."

Otto's feet worked the pedals like he was beating up a cake batter. Closer and faster with every pump.

That was when the mouse darted out from under the front stoop of the grocery. I don't guess grocers cotton to mice a whole lot, so Mr. Rickert threw an empty flowerpot, which almost hit a hen that happened to be pecking the dust. The mouse ducked under Miss Sashay's skirt; and as she screamed, the old hen flapped up toward Goose Gifford.

"Here comes Otto! Real fast."

But old Goose was faster. All he did was finger the cord to ignite the flash powder a bit too early, which caused Mr. Piddle's team of horses to bolt forward just as Otto and his bicycle climbed the ramp at full pedal. Every throat in Chump's Landing yelled or screamed. Instead of over the horses' backs, Otto and his big wheeler crashed through the sheet sign and became the meat of the sandwich. I heard the whole town groan in pain.

Kicking at the hen, Goose said, "Bad birdie."

"Oh, Otto," said Miss Sashay Freshmeadow.

We all ran to the wagon. Except for Goose Gifford, who was chasing the hen; while Mr. McMurtree, with both fists doubled, chased Goose. The hen was little and red, Goose Gifford was tall and lean, and Mr. McMurtree short and stout—it sort of made an interesting race.

At least a couple or three dozen Chump's Landing concerned citizens crowded around the tailgate of Mr. Piddle's wagon in an effort to extract our champion cyclist up and out of the wagon bin. Otto was a tangle of spokes and bruises.

"You hurt, Otto?"

"Somebody go fetch Doc Zirkin."

"I'm right here," said Doc. "Everybody back."

But instead of moving back, we all pressed forward even more, to get ourselves a look-see at what had formerly been a bicycle and a rider.

"I can't look," said Spooner, even though he was staring at the snarl of twisted metal and humiliated humanity.

Otto Piddle's leg was poked through the spokes, his green knickerbockers torn to expose a bleeding knee in front; and in back, a battered buttock.

"Birdies," moaned Otto. "I hear birdies."

"Oh, *no*," said the mayor.

"Let me through," ordered Doc Zirkin.

"Well," said Spooner, "I told ya, Hub."

"Told me what?" I asked.

"I told ya Otto couldn't do it."

"He sure didn't."

Spooner said, "Think he'll try it again?"

I said, "Not before supper."

"Tomorrow?" asked Spooner.

"For gosh sakes," hollered Doc, "will you folks stand aside and let me through?"

Half the folks in town said that Doc Zirkin was the best chiropractor in Chump's Landing. But the other half swore by Doc Kink, who had just arrived on the scene, out of breath and panting. He glowered when he saw Doc Zirkin.

Otto groaned again.

"Mr. Piddle," said Doc Kink, "happens to be *my* patient, so best you folks let *me* take over."

"*Your* patient?" said Doc Zirkin. "Since when?"

"Well," said Doc Kink, "since last year's bicycle race, at which time Otto turned his ankle when dismounting to go to the outhouse. You don't recall?"

"Of course I recall," said Doc Zirkin, "on account it happened to be *my* outhouse."

"But *I* was the one he turned to and *I* was the one who treated him to a free massage. After the race," said Doc Kink.

"That's the root of many a limp in this town," said Doc Zirkin, "and it's all due to massage. Soaking's the answer—in a good hot tub."

"You're all wet, Zirkin," said Doc Kink, "on account water don't cure a cramp. Ask any swimmer."

"Oh, my shinbone," mumbled Otto.

"I don't have to ask a swimmer. Water is Mother Nature's own healer, provided of course you salt the tub-water with half a bottle of my homemade elixir."

"That's an old witch tale if I ever heard one," said Doc Kink. "You and your dangfool elixir-soaking is how Amos Goover contacted water on the knee."

"Amos never got water on the knee. It was a floating kidney. Luckily, my elixir can take a floating kidney and keep it from sinking."

"Somebody help me," Otto gasped.

"Massage is the answer," said Doc Kink.

"Pig's eye! Elixir and water," said Doc Zirkin.

"Elixir? I bet you mix up a batch of that hogwash you call medicine in your wife's laundry tub. No wonder half the town smells of bleach," said Doc Kink.

The two chiropractors stood face to face, toe to toe, at the tailgate of Otto Piddle's wagon. Above their heads, the torn sheet flapped in the warm wind, much of which seemed to be caused by heated conversation.

"Don't you dare," said Doc Zirkin, "to tell *me* how to practice my profession. I got a diploma."

"Yeah, from Sears and Roebuck. I'll have you know that I got a perfect I.Q."

"Perfect? *You?*"

"Right. My I.Q.'s a hundred."

"Huh," snorted Doc Zirkin. "If you got a hundred I.Q., then Goose Gifford's is a thousand."

"Don't you go saying things about Goose," said Doc Kink. "Mr. Gifford happens to be my wife's cousin."

"Your wife's got more than a cousin. She's also got the worst limp in town."

"What of it?"

"And every doggone soul in Chump's Landing knows," said Doc Zirkin, pointing a finger in his colleague's face, "*how* she got it. You practiced night and day on the poor woman while you took that no-good course by mail. It's a wonder Anna didn't die of massage."

"Please," mumbled Otto from beneath his tangled bicycle, "please . . ."

"Massage works wonders," said Doc Kink, "and I got patients all over town who'll bear me witness. Olga Hallerby comes to my office for her weekly adjustment every Wednesday."

"Sure she does. We all seen the poor soul walk to your office. And limp home. The only adjustment *you* oughta make is on your bill."

"Hold on, Zirkin. Olga Hallerby got that limp when she slipped on a mossy rock at the church picnic and fell into Woodson's Crick. That shows what water'll do to a trick knee."

"Ha," said Doc Zirkin. "If you ask me, Woodson's Crick is the only crick in the county that you haven't put in somebody's neck."

"What about *my* knee?" groaned Otto. Half the town groaned too.

"Besides," said Doc Zirkin, "I hear you used to practice your profession in the tackroom of Abe Polaski's livery stable."

"Only while my office was being painted."

"Since when do they need a year to paint up that closet you call an office? Only reason you left Abe's barn was because Abe said your patients were screaming from all that massage, and it spooked the horses."

"And that concoction you call your elixir is made out of no more than maple sap and frog spit."

"Water works wonders. Ask anybody. They'd be a passel of pain in this town if it wasn't for my big soaking tub."

"That's a hot one. You probable *drown* more patients than you cure. The fools who pay you a fee don't need a chiropractor. What *they* need is water wings."

"Help," whispered Otto.

"Horrace..."

My heart leaped. It was an occurrence that sort of happened every time Amoeba May Kiliper spoke my name, which was really Horrace Hubert. The guys called me Hub.

"Good morning, Horrace."

"Howdy," I said. As breakfast almost came up in my throat, I could taste jam and sausage. Love, I thought, was a bit like gastric distress.

"Let's hurry," said Amoeba May, "or we'll be late for school."

She was right. Since it was Monday morning, our being late for school would hardly make the two of us very popular with Miss Guppy. I wanted to walk to school with Amoeba May Kiliper, but I didn't want any of the guys to see me. Especially somebody like Spooner Jitwell. Trouble was, the closer you get to the schoolhouse, the more eyes you run into. That, on top of Amoeba May's always calling me Horrace, was darn near more than my Monday morning could handle.

"Why do you have to call me Horrace?"

"Oh, I guess it's because I think Horrace Hubert is such a *strong* name. Don't you?"

"No, I hate it," I said.

"When I grow up and get married, guess what I'm going to do?"

Here she goes again, I thought, as we walked along Acorn Lane, talking about getting married. "I can't guess," I said.

"I'm going to have a baby."

My cheeks felt suddenly hot. And in my stomach the sausages were frying all over again.

"And," she went on, "if it's a boy, I'm going to name him Horrace."

What a rotten trick, I thought, to pull on a little innocent kid. I was already feeling sorry for Horrace Kiliper.

"Yeah," I said, "but suppose your husband's name is Clyde Finch or Maylander Rizzo, or Albin Hucker?" I named a few more of the guys in our room at school.

"It won't be," said Amoeba.

"How come you already know all that stuff?"

"Because," said Amoeba May, "when I get married, I'm going to be Mrs. Horrace Hubert."

Her steady voice gave me one heck of a jolt.

"You look pale."

"It's worry," I told her, thinking that maybe I best change the subject as quickly as possible.

"Worry over what?"

"Well, I reckon you heard about what happened to Otto Piddle two days ago."

"Certainly I heard," said Amoeba. "It's what my mother and father talked about all day yesterday."

"You're right. People even whispered about Otto in church yesterday morning."

"They did?"

"Yup."

"I heard tell," said Amoeba, as we scooted through the gap in Mrs. O'Hare's back fence, "that Mr. Otto Piddle is going to marry Miss Sashay Freshmeadow. If she works off some weight."

"Let's talk about something else," I said. "Marriage doesn't seem to mix up very smooth with sausages." As I mentioned food, my breakfast seemed to agree. Or rather, to disagree.

"Are you sick, Horrace?"

"No."

"Then why is your hand on your belly?"

"I guess I just feel sorry for Otto, seeing as the Chump's Landing Overland Obstacle Bicycle Race is less than a week off."

"We won't win," said Amoeba. "Daddy says that because Mr. Piddle is now out of the race, this year's winner will be that awful man from Setonville."

"You mean—"

"The one who almost beat Otto last year."

I sighed. "Montana Muldoon."

"Yes," said Amoeba. "That's his name. I remember now, it's Montana Muldoon."

"Well," I said, "even if Otto can't ride his bicycle in

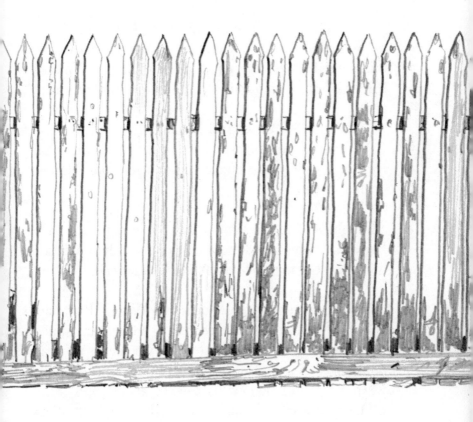

the race, we still have Ernie Kapp. Yeah, and Whitney Mitford."

"*They* won't win," Amoeba said. "My father said that only *two* were just about neck and neck crossing the finish line last year."

"You mean Otto and Muldoon."

"Of course, silly. You saw the race, didn't you?"

"So much of it that I didn't even blink. Ernie came in third, but he was half a mile back. And old Whitney Mitford didn't pump across the finish line until way after dark."

"How come?" Amoeba asked me.

"The way I heard it, Whit took a detour on that final lap. He got his pedals tangled up in a few loose strands of chicken wire."

"Where?"

"Right next to the Widow Bass's hencoop. And then Barnard, her mean old rooster, lit out after him. Chased him so furious that Whit had to hide in the coop."

"Is that all?"

"Nope, there's a whole lot more. Widow Bass happened to be inside her hencoop, harvesting eggs, which she thought poor Whit Mitford had come in to steal. She banged him over the head with a pitchfork. That was when Whit sort of lost his balance and stepped on a rotten floorboard. He sunk one leg down into the floor of the hencoop and couldn't pull it up again. Meanwhile, old Widow Bass kept jabbing him with the fork, and screaming that Whit was a peeping tom and was trying to look up under her skirts."

"Whitney Mitford wouldn't do that."

"Not unless he'd get away with it. As luck would have it, Harv Putnam's sow crawled under the hencoop. I guess that old pig was looking for a cool place in the shade to sleep."

"What did the pig do?"

"Well, as Whit told it, the pig woke up and started to eat his shoe. Harv claims that Alice, that's the name he calls his sow, has the biggest appetite of any pig he ever raised. That was when Whit started yelling, because his foot got bit, and started to swear at the pig. He was yelling "Damn you, Alice.""

"But that's Widow Bass's first name."

I nodded. "That started more trouble, on account that Mrs. Bass thought that Whit Mitford was swearing at her."

"Was he calling her names?"

"Not after she bashed his head with a snow shovel."

"Horrace Hubert?"

"Present."

"Amoeba May Kiliper?"

"Present."

"Spooner Jitwell?"

"Present."

"Clyde Finch?"

"Present."

"Odessa Langford?"

"Present."

"Albin Hucker?"

"Present."

"Maylander Rizzo?"

"Present."

"We're all here," said Miss Guppy in her usual husky

and commanding voice. I figured she sort of had to talk that way at times, as we outnumbered her twenty to one.

Monday morning was hardly ever the most jolly span of my life. Nor anyone else's, I observed, viewing the long faces. Maybe every kid was as worried about Otto Piddle as I was. Even big old Spooner appeared to be a mite troubled, and very little was known to ever worry Spooner Jitwell. He'd think a flood was no more than a heavy dew.

Our teacher, Miss Hossanah Guppenfeffer, opened the top drawer of her desk to tuck away her rollcall book. We hardly ever called her Miss Guppenfeffer. She was Miss Guppy to every kid in Chump's Landing.

"You see," she'd once told us, "lots of folks enjoy having a nickname. My first name is Hossanah, so my brothers called me Hossy until I darn near smelled like one. So to you, I'm just plain Miss Guppy."

I had to admit that it was more fun, and some faster, to call her Miss Guppy as opposed to using Miss Guppenfeffer. Even though she sure didn't look much like that picture of a guppy that Spooner found in an old copy of the *National Geographic*. Our teacher wasn't built much like a guppy. More like a whale. It was probably a toss-up as to who was the biggest soul in town—Otis Dorf, the town blacksmith, or our Miss Guppy.

"Children," said Miss Guppy, "we shall begin our morning study by opening our geography books to page forty-one."

I found page forty-one.

"And," said Miss Guppy, "we shall continue to learn more about the northern territory known as Alaska. Who in the class can tell us how we now lay claim to this ponderous hunk of land?"

"We bought it," said Amoeba May Kiliper.

"Right," said Miss Guppy with an enthusiastic thrust of her fist. "And from *whom* did we buy it, Spooner?"

"Uh, from Rhode Island."

I winced. Scholarship was not one of Spooner's virtues. How I had managed, year after year, to get him promoted was often more than our friendship could endure. Spooner once thought Finland was an aquarium.

"Not quite, Spooner," said Miss Guppy with a sigh. "Are you sure you were paying attention in class last Friday?"

"Yes'm. It was Utah," said Spooner.

"Utah?"

"Well," said Spooner, "it could have been Nebraska. I know all the states, Miss Guppy. Honest. I can name Ohio and Vermont and Italy."

"How about Russia?"

"Russia. Let's see now," said Spooner. "Seems I was trying to remember something about old Russia, but dogged if'n I can recollect too clear."

Clearly, I thought.

"Well," assisted Miss Guppy, "do you recall if Russia once owned Alaska?"

"Yes'm," said Spooner. "I remember now. Russia bought Alaska from Missouri."

Miss Guppy sighed. "Spooner," she said, "try and think."

Obediently, old Spooner clenched his face, a sure sign that he was fixing to crank up his brain.

"It weren't Missouri," he announced.

Wasn't, I silently edited.

"Where?" asked Miss Guppy. "Where, Spooner, did we get Alaska? Think now, and don't be in a *rush*."

"Russia?"

We all clapped. Spooner smiled at the class over his shoulder like the confident geographer he thought he was. I had to give credit to Miss Guppy. She never put old Spooner Jitwell down, even though his brain was his only weak muscle. I saw her wink at Spooner, and he winked back.

"I realize," Miss Guppy said, "that today is a tough time to concentrate. For *all* of us, seeing as Mr. Otto Piddle tangled himself and his vehicle into one awful mess."

I asked, "What about Saturday, Miss Guppy?"

"Ah," she answered, "that's our problem, isn't it? Who's going to ride a bicycle for Chump's Landing now that Otto busted himself up?"

"We got Ernie," said Spooner.

Have, I thought.

"Yes," said Miss Guppy. "Last year, both Ernie Kapp and Whitney Mitford pedaled a noble race. Trouble is, Setonville has Montana Muldoon."

We all moaned.

The very mention of Muldoon's name was enough to darken a Monday morning even further. I remembered Montana Muldoon from last year. His arms were bigger than most men's legs. Some folks from Setonville said that Mr. Muldoon had once worked in a traveling tent show, as a weight lifter. He was baldheaded; and on his upper lip, he sported a big black handlebar mustache, bulky as bullhorns. Otto Piddle had a red mustache, but *his* smiled.

"What are we going to do, Miss Guppy?"

"Now that you ask," said Miss Guppy, "I think that tonight, when we all are getting ready to go to sleep, we should offer up a little prayer for Mr. Piddle."

"What kind of a prayer?" asked Amoeba.

"Just make it short and sweet, in your own words, because prayers you make up yourselves are the best kind. Straight from *your* heart up to the Almighty's."

"Are you going to pray, too, Miss Guppy?"

"Bet your boots I am. But we can't leave everything to Heaven. Best we do some thinking ourselves if we plan to win the trophy this Saturday."

"What'll we do, Miss Guppy?"

"I sure wish I knew, Odessa. We better hustle up a fresh idea, or Montana Muldoon is going to strut off with our silver cup."

Closing my eyes, I saw the dark face of Mr. Montana Muldoon as he received congratulations last year for finishing in second place. All he got was a red ribbon from Mayor Smather. I saw Montana eye the big silver trophy that Otto won. And more, I also saw Mr. Muldoon staring, bold as you please, at no other lady than Miss Sashay Freshmeadow. He looked her up and looked her down, twisting the ends of his black mustache.

"Yes indeedy," said Miss Guppy, "we best *do* something prior to the Chump's Landing Overland Obstacle Bicycle Race, and we only have five more days to do it."

"Do what, Miss Guppy?"

"First off, we have to find a substitute, a stand-in for Mr. Piddle. Because our friend Otto can't ride."

"He can't?"

"No, not with his puffed-up knee," said Miss Guppy. "Poor Mr. Piddle wouldn't be able to pedal ten feet."

"Is that all we do, find a substitute?"

Miss Guppy shook her head, her lips grimly set with determination. "That's just the beginning. We need an overall plan. After we find our new bicyclist, *then* we figure out how he'll win. But first, we've *got* to find a good rider."

Spooner raised his hand.

"Yes, Spooner?"

"I know a real good rider."

"*Who?*" asked Miss Guppy.

Spooner smiled. "Montana Muldoon."

"Hurry," said Spooner.

Even though we were in no particular rush, I hurried, dropping my arithmetic book, which made me scoot back a few paces to retrieve it.

"Now what?"

"Well, I dropped my book in the mud." I brushed some topsoil off a triangle and an ellipse.

"Tough luck, Hub."

"Darn it. Something like this always happens when we run home from school."

"Cheer up," said Spooner. "Last month, I dropped my report card in Dewey's Swamp, when we took the shortcut."

That's where Spooner Jitwell's report card belonged. In a swamp. I began to have nagging doubts of my ability to get Spooner much past elementary school. He hardly ever read a book. Except one. I knew as a fact that he had secretly started *Heidi* on fourteen different occasions.

"Hub—"

"Yeah?"

"We got ourselves two whole hours from now until choretime. Let's not fritter it all away on grooming your arithmetic."

"Okay," I said, wiping off multiplication tables with my red bandana. "By the way, Spooner—how much is seven times seven?"

Spooner's face looked blanker than a collection plate on a rainy Sunday. "I don't guess I know."

I said, "Take a stab at it."

Spooner stabbed. "Is it fifty-two?"

"Wrong."

"Am I warm?"

"Sort of."

"Something's fifty-two," said Spooner.

"Right," I said. "Four times thirteen."

"Fifty-two?"

"Yup," I said.

Spooner grinned. "Clubs, diamonds, hearts, and spades. Thirteen each, because there's fifty-two cards in a pack. I counted 'em."

An idea suddenly got born in my brain. "Hey, Spooner, do you still have that deck of cards?"

"Right in my pocket, like usual."

"Yank 'em out."

"Hub, you wanna play Black Jack?"

"Sort of. Maybe a new version."

"For pennies?"

"Well," I said, "I would, but I don't happen to have any pennies right now."

"Shucks. Neither do I."

Setting myself down on a nail keg just outside Mr. Vinner's tannery, I motioned for Spooner to do likewise on the other keg. A barrel was between us, flat end up.

"Fetch out the cards," I said.

"For what?"

"A new game."

"I gotta warn ya, Hub. You know I usual whack the pants off you at cards."

"You sure do," I said. "My deal."

Shuffling cards belonging to Spooner Jitwell was no cinch. Instead of being white, the cards were grayer than old Vint Bozarth's laundry, especially his dingy old underwear that flapped out on the line for near a week. The kings, queens, and jacks were so beat up that they looked about as much like royalty as the hobo gang who camped by the railroad tracks. Each card was bent floppier than a leaf a lettuce. So shuffling came close to tossing a salad.

I dropped a red queen.

"What's the game?" Spooner asked.

"It's called Rabbit," I lied. Not really a lie. The game had a lot to do with multiplying.

Spooner wrinkled his nose. "How's it go?"

I dealt out two sevens, a four, and a nine, placing them faceup on the barrelhead so's they'd read from Spooner's left to his right. Pointing at each of the four cards in turn, I said "Seven times seven is . . ." and waited.

"Four nine," said Spooner. "Forty-nine."

"Bully for you."

"You call this a game?"

"Well, I bet you can *beat* me once you learn all the tricks."

"Learn me another, Hub."

"I'll *teach* you another. *You* will learn."

"Hey," said Spooner, holding up his big dirty fist, "you aren't about to start *correcting* the way I talk again. Are ya?"

"Not me." I swallowed, as old Spooner's knuckles had powers of persuasion all their own. Dealing out an eight, nine, seven, and two of spades, I again pointed to the cards. "Eight times nine . . ."

"Is seven two—seventy-two. Hub, this ain't no game. All it is is schoolwork." Spooner yawned.

"What if it is?"

"I've had enough of school and enough of Miss Guppy. She can take Alaska and shove it back into Russia."

"At least you got *that* right."

"Know what, Hub?"

"Tell me." I shuffled the cards again, waiting to hear Spooner Jitwell's next statement.

"Honest to gosh, Hub, in a few years when I get to be fourteen, I'm going to quit school."

"Ya can't."

"Oh yes I can. You can quit school soon as you turn fourteen. It's a state law."

"Now look, Spooner. You'd be the last guy in Chump's Landing to pay heed to any *law* that was ever passed. You're always saying that your pa's got a right to cook up a batch of corn whisky, law or no law. Right?"

"Right."

"Then how come," I asked Spooner, "you gotta bow your head in reverence and take off your cap to some dumb *law* that says you can quit school soon as you hit fourteen?"

"I'm quitting, Hub. And that's final."

"No you're not. I won't let you. You're going to knuckle in and stick. Without an education, Miss Guppy said, no kid holds a prayer of nailing down a steady job."

"Who'd hire *me*?"

"Lots of people."

"I'm dumb, Hub."

"But you're *not*. You're a better poker player now than I'll *ever* be."

"Honest?"

"Sure. And if you can figure out the arithmetic of Black Jack, which you already have, you can add and subtract and multiply and divide and do fractions, enough to work at Rickert's Grocery or at Quimby's Drygoods, or darn near all over town."

"Just maybe Miss Guppy's right, Hub."

Saying nothing, I dealt Spooner a six, nine, five, and four of hearts. "What's six times nine?"

"Five four—fifty-four."

"Easy, huh?" I asked Spooner.

"Yeah, but the nine-times sure are tough. Eights are a leadpipe cinch compared to them cussed nines."

Those cussed nines, I said, silently so as not to press my luck or ruin my health.

"Nines," I said, "are the easiest. That's because the answer always adds up to nine."

"I don't get it."

"Look." I dealt out two red nines and two black nines. Then some random cards to multiply them. "See?"

"Keep talking."

"Five times nine is forty-five. The four and five in your answer add up to nine."

"Yeah. So it do."

"And when nine times seven is sixty-three, the six and three make nine as a total. It's sort of a check I use to make sure I'm right, whenever I multiply by nine."

"Golly," said Spooner.

"Nine times nine is eighty-one, and the eight and one make . . ."

"Nine."

"A snap." I smiled at Spooner and he smiled at me. He had an apple pie for a face, big and round, freckles and sandy hair that was straighter than straw.

"Thanks a lot, Hub."

"Forget it. Let's play cards."

"Naw." Spooner reached a chubby hand into a tight pocket to fish out a pair of green dice with white spots, which he rattled inside his fist. Then he made his suggestion.

"Let's shoot craps. The numbers are smaller."

-6-

The next day, Tuesday, turned out to be better than most, because Miss Guppy had to attend a county teachers meeting. So she chased us out of school at noon.

"See ya later, Hub."

"Where ya headed?" I asked Spooner.

"Fishing, with my old man. You can tag along if you want to go home and fetch your pole," Spooner said, "long as you don't talk arithmetic every breath and spook the trout."

"Thanks," I said, "but I got matters to do."

"Like what?"

"Well, I best do some brain figuring about the bicycle race on Saturday."

"So long."

"Bye."

Leaving old Spooner, I stopped in at Piddle's Pedals, the bicycle shop, to check the health of Mr. Otto Piddle. His knee must have been bandaged, according to the bulge in his trouser leg, and his arm was in a sling. His walk could hardly be described as spry. He limped some.

"Howdy there, Hub."

"Howdy, Mr. Piddle."

"What can I do ya for?"

"Well, I sort of stopped by to inquire about your health and general well-being."

Otto Piddle smiled. "I'll mend," he said, "but not prior to Saturday, doggone it."

I tried to smile. Yet all I could think about was the forthcoming Chump's Landing Overland Obstacle Bicycle Race, a contest that we could never win without Otto Piddle to pedal his big yellow bike. Right now, that was the very same vehicle that Otto was working on. It's condition could hardly be described as hardy.

"I'm sorry," I told Otto.

"Guess I'd be hard pressed," said Otto, pointing a wrench at me, "to determine which one of us is in sorrier shape. Me, or my bike."

Both of them looked a mite bent.

"Who can ride for Chump's Landing?" I asked.

"I guess Ernie, or Whit."

"Do they have a chance?"

"Hub, that's not for me to say. They're a pair of good old boys, and if they can gang up on Muldoon, maybe one of them can pump under that old finish line first."

"Mr. Piddle . . ."

"Uh huh."

"How fast is Montana Muldoon?"

"Hub, I sure hate to admit it. And I sure wouldn't want it to get around, but I best confess he's a spoke or two faster than I am."

"Faster than *you?*"

"Yup. Sure is."

"*Nobody's* faster than you, Mr. Piddle."

"Whoa. Ya see, Hub, no matter how fast a feller burns a bike, there's *always* somebody that can pump a turn or two faster. Muldoon's strong and he rides dirty."

"Then how come, last year, *you* managed to beat Muldoon?"

Before answering Otto wiped his hands on a cheese-cloth. "The way I got it pegged, Montana Muldoon is faster on a straightaway. But not around curves. Snaking around a bend, Muldoon and I race about even-Steven. Except when he crowds me off into the ditch."

"You sure?"

Mr. Piddle nodded.

"But you edged him out at the finish line."

Otto grinned, turning up the tips of his red mustache so that it smiled, too. I liked Otto's face. And he never seemed too busy to talk to any kid who stopped by, like me, who dreamed about being a famous cyclist. And a clean rider.

"Yeah," said Otto, "I edged him. But it was maybe more luck than skill."

"How come?"

"Hub, a bike race around a track is one thing. But an overland race, with obstacles, is another kettle of fish."

"In what way?"

"A smart rider is one that uses his *head* as well as his feet. Pick your spot, for example, where you cycle through a shallow crickbed. Muldoon pulled a big boner last year, when he picked the steepest path down the bank to cross Woodson's Crick."

"Did he?"

"Right as rain he did. Speed isn't everything. Steep banks hurry your bike more, true enough, but steep banks also mean that the crick narrows, and *that's* where the water's deeper. Trips your spokes."

"What do *you* do?"

"Me? I pick the widest part of the crick to cross through, where the water is so shallow that you can darn near read the freckles on the pebbles."

I liked to hear Otto talk. Everything he said was real friendly, and I was sort of thankful that Miss Sashay Freshmeadow was sweet on him.

Mr. Piddle removed a broken spoke, tossing the two lengths of wire into his box of scrap. As he wrestled to unbend the yellow rim, I nosed around the bicycle shop. Three new bicycles had just come in: red, green, and pink. Each had silver trim all the way around the big front wheel, on the frame, and along the handlebars. Running my hand along the iron was sort of like being allowed to touch an angel's harp. With my thumbnail, I rippled the spokes, just to hear the notes of music.

I picked up a pair of racing goggles.

"Try 'em on, Hub."

"Honest? I can?"

"Go ahead. Let's see how you look."

The goggles slipped over my head, pinching in my curly hair; they felt a bit loose until I hitched in the strap a notch or two.

"There's a mirror over yonder."

"Thanks," I said.

The kid I saw in the mirror was only Horrace Hubert from the nostrils down. Up above, I looked like a regular grown-up bicycle racer. The goggles were black with red trim.

"Wow!" I said.

"You look right spiffy," said Otto.

"I do?"

"Like a real champeen racer."

"Honest?"

"Honest injun."

"Mr. Piddle, is it okay if I climb up on one of your *used* bikes and sit on the seat, and pretend?"

"No," said Otto.

My heart sort of sank.

"Here ya go, Hub." Before I could see too much out of the goggles, Otto lifted me up onto the seat of the red bicycle. "A polite boy like you deserves to sit on this *new* beauty."

He sure was strong, even if his arm was in a sling and his knee probable hurt.

"Boy! Oh gosh, Mr. Piddle, thanks a whole lot."

"Now then, soon as your legs sprout a bit, and get long enough so's your feet can reach both pedals, I just might—"

"*Teach* me?"

"You bet."

"I don't guess I can wait."

Grabbing the handgrips, I leaned forward, almost feeling the wind of downhill speed whistling into my face, against my goggles, even though there wasn't enough breeze in Otto's shop to snuff out a birthday candle.

"I wish, I wish, I wish . . ."

Mr. Piddle hung on to me and the bicycle so I wouldn't tip over. I sure was up high.

"That's the way of it, Hub. Same when I was a kid your size. At times, it doesn't seem like a boy will ever grow up and be a man. Nothing but schoolwork, spanks, and chores. Then, before you can turn around and blink, you sprout up tall and handsome."

"Like a weed," I said.

"Hub, I hope that if I ever get wed, that my wife and I spawn a boy just like you."

"Gee, Mr. Piddle. I don't guess I know what to say."

"Well, you're already starting to grow up so doggone fast, best you start today to say something brand new."

"Like what?"

"From now on, you don't have to be calling me Mr. Piddle anymore. After all, I'm not so old as all that. I'm only twenty-five."

"What do I call you, Mr. Piddle?"

"I call you Hub. You call me Otto."

"Thanks, Otto. Thanks a whole bagfull."

"Unless you prefer Horrace."

I saw Spooner.

No sooner had I left Otto's bicycle shop and headed for home, I spotted Spooner Jitwell trudging through Mrs. Kelloway's garden, his bare feet jumping over a row of radishes. A long whippy fishpole of bamboo was over his shoulder. He wasn't toting any trout.

"Hub!"

"Hey, I thought you were going fishing."

"I did go."

"Weren't they biting?"

"Nope."

"Where's your pa?" I asked Spooner.

"Oh, I left him under a sassafras tree, fast asleep, down by the crick. Pa said that seeing as the trout all seemed to be napping, he'd do it, too."

"That makes sense to me."

"What'll we do, Hub? Be a cussed shame to waste a sunny afternoon."

"I got an idea."

"Like what?" Spooner sat himself down on an old stump to scratch his bug bites.

"Well," I said, "what say we scout the race course?"

"What for?"

"Obstacles."

"What kind of obstacles, Hub?"

"Appears to me," I said, "we best spot a place or two where Montana Muldoon just might pedal his bike into a tub of trouble."

Spooner smiled. "Now you're talking."

"Come on."

"Where?"

"Oh, for a starter, let's draw a map."

"A map?"

"Spooner, remember what Miss Guppy always tells us."

"Yeah, I recall. Most of the time she tells you and me to hush up."

"Miss Guppy says that it's important to noodle up an overall plan, whether you're writing a poem or just doing chores."

Spooner nodded. "That's funny. I guess I thought her overall plan was sort of a blueprint for sewing up overalls."

"So, seeing as Miss Guppy is usual right about most

things, best we take her advice and map out our plan."

"What'll we aim to do?"

"Well, come Saturday, you and I are going to prevent Montana Muldoon and his dirty tricks from winning the Chump's Landing Overland Obstacle Bicycle Race."

"How?"

In my arithmetic book was a spare sheet of white paper, which I pulled out. I started to draw with the stub of a crayon.

"I give up," said Spooner, watching me rub out a mistake with my pink eraser. "All you seem to be drawing is a mess."

"This here," I pointed at my paper, "is a map of our town."

"You mean *that* is Chump's Landing?"

"Uh huh," I said with a nod. "And this," I drew a big yellow oval around the outside, "is the race course."

"Looks more like a squash."

"Right here," I told Spooner, "is the first turn."

"That's at Goose Gifford's shack."

"Check," I said. "And that's the place Goose sometimes is feeding cracked corn to every goose he owns."

"Right near the path of the bike racers?"

"But not *all* the racers."

"You mean only Montana Muldoon?"

I smiled. "Not even Mr. Muldoon can pedal a bike through a flock of Goose Gifford's geese."

"Not when they're all loose as a goose," said Spooner, who was starting to become part of my plan.

"Next," I said, working on my map, "the track runs by Elva Watson's place. You know that Mrs. Watson takes in wash. There's got to be an extra clothesline strung up."

"About neck high." Spooner chuckled.

"Right. Then there's Dobson's Hill. Otto said that a racer has to pedal real fast to get a start up that grade."

"Or else jump off and push."

"So we slow Muldoon down,"—I pointed at my map—"right about here."

"Where's that?"

"Harv Putnam's pigpen."

"Old Harv doesn't cotton to folks messing around with his porkers," said Spooner.

"No," I agreed, "I don't guess he does. However, he just might get a giggle when he sees a pig or two messing around with Muldoon."

"Harv," said Spooner, "ain't one to giggle much. Then what?"

My map was already looking more like a pigsty than Harv's property, yet I kept on drawing, erasing, and re-drawing the bicycle race course as best as my crayon stubs would allow. Spooner leaned in close. Wow, that Jitwell kid sure could have used a bath. Pointing an un-soaped finger on my map, he asked me a question.

"Hub, what are all those little red triangles?"

"My red triangles," I said, "just happen to be the most important items on this whole map."

"Well, what are they, Hub?"

"Flags."

Spooner snapped his dirty fingers. "Of course. The red flags they use to mark the race track."

"You got it."

"But the judges plant the red flags in the same spots every year, don't they, Hub?"

"More or less," I said. "Not always. Yet they're allowed to change a flag's position *during* a race."

"What if you and I pull up a flag or two?"

"That," I told Spooner, "is just what we aim to do."

"Where'll we move 'em to? And *how?*" Spooner whipped his fishpole in the air, which gave me a fresh inspiration.

"Ice fish," I said.

"Huh?"

"Spoon, I just got one beauty of an idea! And it's all because you went fishing today."

The look on Spooner Jitwell's face told me that, for the moment, I was way ahead of him. "Hub, I sure don't understand how a bike race is kin to ice fish. Besides, winter's long gone."

"Think," I said, "what your pa does with his fishing shanty every December."

"Well," said Spooner, "soon as the ice on the lake freezes thick enough, we push it out on the ice so we can hide from the wind. You oughta know, Hub. We both been ice fishing plenty of winters."

"Right. And we can't ice fish without a tip-up, can we?"

"Sure we could. But the tip-up lies flat over the hole in the ice until a fish bites the bait."

"And then," I said, "a little red flag pops up, no more than a foot or so high."

Spooner's face lit up brighter than a cellar lantern. "I get it. The judges mark the course with the same kind of red flags. Tip-up flags."

"Right," I said. "The flag isn't cloth. It's only a little wooden triangle on the top end of a stake that they jam in the ground."

"So what do we do?"

"Easy," I said. "The officials mark out the race course a day or two early, before the race. So what we'll do is doctor up a few of the flags so that they'll tip up, or fall flat and out of sight."

Spooner smiled. His face told me how much he'd usually cotton to just about any kind of caper that had the smell of trickery. Then his expression darkened into the type of frown that he so often reserved for a spelling test.

"Hub, we forgot something."

"We did?"

"Yeah. Something important."

"Like what?" I asked him.

"Now that we got the race all figured out, to how Montana Muldoon is going to *lose*, we gotta noodle out one more detail."

"And what's that?"

"Seems to me," said Spooner, "we ought to figure out *who's* going to *win*."

"Yeah," I said, "and as I got it figured, we're going to need one more very important item."

"Like what?"

"A tub."

"Strike three!" said Miss Guppy.

Behind the schoolhouse in the vacant lot, we were all playing our usual noontime game of baseball, umpired by Miss Guppenfeffer.

"Doggone it," said Spooner, "why do I strike out so much?"

Spooner scowled at Odessa Langford, a gal who happened to be the fastest pitcher in the whole school. She could strike out Spooner Jitwell on three straight pitches, and did most every day. I had a hunch that Spooner was looking at Odessa instead of the ball.

"Time out," said Miss Guppy.

"How come?"

"Because," said Miss Guppy, "it doesn't make a very

exciting baseball game if Odessa strikes out all you boys every time you come to the plate."

"What'll we do?" asked Spooner.

"Watch me," said Miss Guppy. With the bat over her right shoulder, she stepped up to home plate. "Notice," she said, "my feet. Take a stance about as wide as your shoulders."

Miss Guppy's stance was considerably wider than the footprints that Spooner's bare feet had left in the dust. Everything about our teacher was wide, including her smile, as she faced Odessa Langford. I couldn't see the plate. Miss Guppy's broad expanse even blotted out most of the catcher, Betsy Barney.

"Now then," said Miss Guppy, "notice how I get the bat *off* my shoulder when I'm ready to hit. Bat back, and weight back on my right foot. Start your swing early, on *every* delivery. If it's a fat pitch, follow through with your bat, and swing *through* the ball. Don't chop at it, Spooner. Baseball's different than splitting kindling."

"Yes'm," said Spooner.

"Next," said Miss Guppy, "you best remember what we learned this morning in geography."

"Geography?"

"Right. Horrace, when you look at our globe, where's the Equator?"

"Right around the middle. The fat part."

"Good." Miss Guppy's chubby hand held the sponge-rubber ball that was the color of rust. "And you, Betsy—where's the Northern Hemisphere?"

"The top half," said Betsy.

"Correct. So when you swing a bat, take your cut at the top half of the ball, at North America or Siberia."

"How about Argentina?" said Spooner.

"Ah ha!" said Miss Guppy. "That's your problem at the plate, Spooner. Swing low, and your bat passes under the ball. Or you hit a pop-up."

"Honest?"

"Another thing," said Miss Guppy as she tossed the ball out to Odessa on the mound, "keep that right elbow up a mite."

"What's it do?"

"It'll level out your swing. All right now, Odessa. Let's see your high hard one, right over the plate. Burn it in. Over the old pan."

Odessa Langford spit on her hand, gripped the ball, reared back, and fired her sizzler, a pitch that could have struck out Mr. Abner Doubleday himself, who invented baseball. Bat back, Miss Guppy was more than prepared. Stepping into the pitch with her left foot, her bat met the ball.

Splat!

Just over the fence beyond left field, I saw Eunice, who was Mr. Hapgood's milk cow. I didn't think that even the homerun hero of the whole world could hit a ball as far as Eunice. Then it landed, beyond the fence, and bounced to a stop against the buttercup that Eunice was about to eat. I heard the clank of a surprised cowbell.

"Wow!" said Spooner. "See that, Hub?"

I only nodded, as to speak at such a moment would have sort of come close to being irreverent. Like burping in church. Then we ran out to where left field ended. As we got to the fence, there was our rubber ball, resting comfortable in the green meadowgrass in front of Eunice.

"Somebody better get it," said Miss Guppy, but nobody raised a hand to volunteer. Resting one foot on the bottom rail of the fence, she pointed at the ball. "Well, who's going to climb over and fetch it?"

We all were quite silent, except for Eunice's cowbell which clanked out a warning.

"Spooner?"

"I would, Miss Guppy, but I'm not too sure about Eunice."

"Hmm," said Miss Guppy, "Eunice looks gentle enough to me."

Chewing slowly, Eunice stared quietly at all of us, moving one of her hefty hoofs a step closer to our ball. I didn't trust Eunice; neither the sleepy look in her soft brown eyes nor her long and curly horns. Somehow she seemed to know that left field was ours, but "over the fence" was hers. Her tail whipped a fly.

"Good afternoon, Eunice," I said. A big error.

"How about it, Hub?" asked Miss Guppy. "Think you can scamper over the fence and retrieve our ball?"

No, I thought. I can't. Then I remembered Miss Guppy's general attitude about kids who say "I can't." Unfavorable. But my feet sort of felt glued to the grass of safety.

Spooner said, "I don't guess Hub wants to."

"Do *you?*" I asked Spooner.

"Not a whole lot."

"Well," said Miss Guppenfeffer, "*somebody* has to get it. Reckon it ought to be me, seeing as it was my bat that smacked it there in the first place."

Before we could stop her, Miss Guppy lifted up her skirts. Over the fence she went. I didn't envy our teacher. Sharing a pasture with Eunice was hardly my idea of a Sunday picnic. Yet I'll say this for Miss Guppy. She was not the type of person who allowed herself to be afraid of things, or cows.

Eunice's bell clanked a few times as she tossed her head in Miss Guppy's direction.

Bending low, Miss Guppy picked a fresh handful of clover that grew under the shade of the fencepost. "Here," she said as she aproached the cow and the ball. "Nice girl."

Spooner Jitwell whispered into my ear. "Ya know, Hub, I always picture Miss Guppy as being so doggone big. But not today."

"No," I agreed, "not compared to Eunice."

"Nice cow," said Miss Guppy, slowly advancing toward the ball that now lay between two large front hoofs.

"Hub," said Spooner, "I wouldn't go near old Eunice for all the pie in the pantry."

"Me neither. Not if she'd been dead for a week."

To me, it appeared that Eunice didn't admire the sprig of clover that Miss Guppy was holding. Eunice also had a look in her eye that sort of professed that she didn't care about Miss Guppy either. Or baseball. Eunice lowered her head, then raised up, staring directly at our teacher. We knew how strong Miss Guppy was; but I had to admit that Eunice Hapgood appeared to be at least half a ton stronger.

"Please be careful, Miss Guppy," said Amoeba May Kiliper. To my ear, it sounded like a right sensible suggestion. Amoeba May was standing right beside me, peeking over the top rail of the gray wooden fence.

"Want some clover, Eunice?" asked Miss Guppy in a gentle voice. "It's real sweet."

Eunice didn't want any clover. What she suddenly wanted was Miss Guppenfeffer. Bell clanking and horns lowered, she moved forward. It wasn't really an all-out charge. More of a confident walk. A thousand pounds of milk cow add up to one heck of a hunk of confidence.

"*Now*," ordered Miss Guppy as she backed away from Eunice, "somebody climb over here and grab the ball."

"You go," said Amoeba May into my ear.

"Me?"

"You're not *afraid*, are you?"

"Not on *this* side of the fence."

"Horrace Hubert," said Amoeba May Kiliper, "you don't want me to think you're a scaredy-cat, do you?"

"No," I said, looking at Eunice's two horns and four hoofs. And her cowbell that was big enough to hang in Philadelphia.

"Then do it."

I did it. *Why*, I asked myself as I climbed over the fence, am I going to kill myself for a ball? Then I reasoned out the answer. I was doing it for Miss Guppy and for Amoeba May Kiliper, and because I didn't want Eunice to hurt our teacher. I ran. Eunice turned just as I reached the ball. That was when my foot slipped on a pie of fresh cowdung.

"Look out," yelled Amoeba May.

I tried to grab the ball and get up at the same time, accomplishing neither.

"Run," commanded Miss Guppy.

But I didn't. Instead I got to my feet just as Eunice was returning to insist that the ball was now hers, but I still couldn't seem to locate it. That was because it was so hard to grab a ball when your eyes keep looking at cow horns. And hearing an angry cowbell.

"I got it!" I said. But old Eunice was now between me and the fence.

"Here now, Eunice," said Miss Guppy.

As the cow turned to our teacher, I ran for the fence. Eunice snorted a warning. The kids all screamed. Ripping my trousers on the top rail, I tumbled over to safety. Then I turned back to see a miracle. With a running start, Miss Guppy vaulted over the fence as easily as you'd skip over a ladybug.

"Glad I'm an athlete," our teacher said.

"Miss Guppy," said Amoeba May Kiliper, "can you ride a bicycle?"

I stayed after school.

Spooner had extra chores to mind, so I told him that I'd see him after supper. The Jitwells worked a farm just uproad from where we Huberts lived.

"Feeling sick?" Miss Guppy asked me.

"No, Miss Guppy. I just thought I'd empty the waste basket and wash the blackboard for you, that's all. It's sort of my turn."

"Thank you, Horrace. You're a willing lad."

"I sort of have something to talk about, that is if you can spare the time."

"So I figured. Shoot."

"Well," I said, "I just wanted to start off by saying that you're a brave teacher."

"Thank you, Horrace. I do appreciate your saying it. But no braver than you."

"I don't guess," I said, "that I really thought a *teacher* would climb a fence and fetch a ball. Especially since Eunice was so nearby."

Miss Guppy smiled. I finished the blackboards and we stepped outside to sit on the wooden bench that leaned against the hip of the schoolhouse. My teacher produced an orange that was left over from her lunchbox, which she peeled with her fingers, handing me a half. "Have a hemisphere," she said.

"Thanks," I said. Then I repeated about how she vaulted over Mr. Hapgood's fence, in left field.

"Being a schoolmarm," she said, "can mean one fence after another. So what's one more?"

I didn't understand, and I reckon my face told her so. My hand scratched my ear.

"By that," she said, "I mean that we teachers are akin to bicycle racers."

"How so?"

"Before us, in our path, there are always obstacles aplenty. Some fences you can vault over. Yet other fences seem high as a rainbow."

"What sort of fences?"

"Well, for example, when a schoolmarm helps herself to a sip of cider at a barn dance, there's always some busybody to wonder if the cider is hard or sweet."

"I understand. Sort of the way they spy on preachers."

"Fences," said Miss Guppy. "Even if you're cautious, folks erect rails around a teacher until she's boxed in too tight to even draw a free breath of either life or liberty."

"Do you like cider?" I asked her.

"Bet I do. A swallow of cider with a kick to it can be mighty good for fending off a chest cold. And a swig of tart cider makes a good dancer prance a step or two merrier."

"I don't know how to dance."

"Well, maybe for the time being, that's not quite one of your problems. Is it?"

"Yes'm, because Amoeba May Kiliper says she's fixing to teach me."

"Good. Then learn. It may come in useful."

"Do you like to barn-dance?"

As an answer, Miss Guppy's big hand clapped me on the shoulder. "Sure I do. But when a schoolteacher dances, big as I am, there's more than one tongue in town that'll wag along with my waddle."

"Don't folks want you to have any fun?"

"Not much. And that's the straight of it. I can honestly guess that a good many people think I ought to stay home and knit. Or feed the cat."

"And that's all?"

Miss Guppy nodded. "You see, Hub, I have a gentleman friend who comes calling every weekend. He's from north of Setonville."

"Is that Harry?"

"Yes. Know him?"

"We shook hands once. He has one heck of a strong grip. And he sure is a big fellow. Big as Montana Muldoon."

"Bigger. And lots sweeter."

"Are you going to get married?"

"Who knows? But whether I do or don't, it really shouldn't worry anyone except Harry or me. I've been sort of sweet on old Harry for, let's see now, most of a good ten years."

"Ten years. Wow."

"Not so long, the way time slips by. How long have you been sweet on Amoeba May Kiliper?"

I felt my face turn red. As my cheeks roasted up, I almost covered my face with my hands.

"Loving somebody," said Miss Guppy, "is naught to blush bashful about. It's to be proud of, like a banner or a flag that you hold up real high for the whole world to salute."

I nodded. "I guess that's sort of the way I feel about Amoeba May. But it's a secret."

"Good lad. Continue to feel that way always, if your heart's so inclined. I tell you, Hub, there's two kinds of folks in every county."

"Two kinds?"

"First, there are the people who love, bless their happy souls."

"What about the second kind?"

"The other crowd is made up of folks too empty to love. So they point fingers at a pair of people who hold hands, or send valentines, or play post office, or just plain spark in the moonlight."

"I'm not very handy at kissing."

"Who says?"

"Amoeba May Kiliper."

"What makes you think *she's* an expert?"

"Well, maybe she's not an expert compared to a grown-up sparker, but she sure is mighty learned compared to me."

As I talked, orange juice ran down my chin. Taking out her hanky from her sleeve, Miss Guppy wiped my chin, which made the linen turn a bit brown. My face must have blotted up some topsoil. Or some cowdung from beyond left field.

"Better?"

I nodded. "Thanks. How come you wanted to become a schoolmarm?"

"Had to be."

"If you had it to do over, now that you know about—you know, all the fences and obstacles—would you still become a teacher?"

"Bet your boots, Hub. Your pa's a farmer, eh?"

"Yes'm, he is. We both are."

"Farmers and teachers are sisters under the skin, to borrow a phrase from a poet, name of Rudyard Kipling. A teacher, like a farmer, has a fresh green garden that skips into her life each morning. A garden to be tended and nursed. And I often have to weed out a few bad habits."

"Like when you caught Spooner and me chewing tobacco."

"Yessir, and you both got my ruler for a whack or two, right on the place where it did the most good."

"You gave me two whacks," I said, "but you gave old Spooner three."

"That was because it was *his* tobacco."

"How did *you* know that?"

Miss Guppy winked. "A day will come, Hub, when you'll be pleasantly surprised as to just how much we teachers learn in school."

"I reckon you know a whole lot of stuff."

"You mean about arithmetic, geography, or subjects of similar breed?"

"Yes'm. But other stuff, too."

"Such as?"

"Fences." As I said it, I hoped she knew that I meant the fences like barn dancing, or cider.

Miss Guppy looked at me, not speaking, just sort of staring into my eyes. When she finally spoke, her voice was low and soft, and sweet as candy.

"Hub, I'm real glad."

"Yes'm. Glad about what?"

"I'm right grateful you're growing in my garden."

Her hand touched my face. Then she went inside to get a needle and thread. I lay across her lap while she sewed up a rip in the seat of my trousers.

"Hub," she said as she finally bit the thread, "you never got around to asking me."

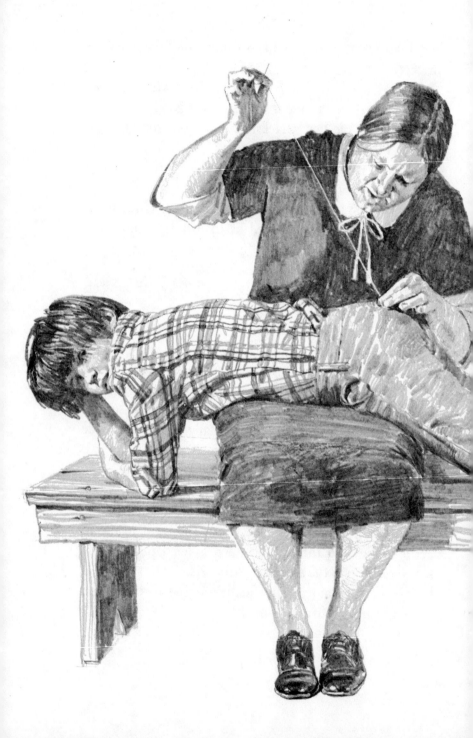

"No," I said, "I don't guess I did."

"Are you going to? After all, that was the prime purpose in your staying after school, wasn't it?"

"Yes. But I don't have to now."

"No," said Miss Guppy, "because the answer is yes. I'll give 'er a try."

"You'll *do* it?"

"You bet I'll do it."

I said, "I've never seen you ride a bicycle, so I figured maybe you didn't know how."

"Every brother I have was, and still is, bicycle crazy, and Harry used to ride some before he sprained his ankle. So I guess I'm more than qualified. I can ride."

"Montana Muldoon," I said, "here we come."

"I found one," yelled Spooner.

He was out of breath from running, hot and sweaty, yet with a wide grin across his face. I looked down from the lower limb of the maple tree behind Amos Groover's barn. My hands were black from climbing, and I was on the way down. When my feet hit the ground, I sat in the shade to hear old Spooner tell his tale.

"You really found one, Spooner?"

"I certain did."

"Where?"

"It wasn't easy," Spooner said, as we sat side by side under the tree, "because they're scarce as hen's teeth. Unless you poke around in bed chambers."

"Well, where is it?"

"Soon as I catch my breath," said Spooner, "I'll give ya a full report. You won't believe it, Hub."

I could tell that Spooner Jitwell was enjoying the fact that he knew something that I was still in the dark about. He sure loved to play this game, so I just blew the seeds off a dandelion ball and waited for him to crank up his story.

"Up the ridge," said Spooner.

"Keep talking."

"I was sneaking along through the hedge behind Olga Hallerby's house, and then I ducked under a hole in the fence."

"That's where Doc Zirkin lives."

"Right. Now listen, Hub. It was in Doc's backyard where I found it."

"No kidding."

"It was shining in the sunlight, all bright and coppery, right there in plain sight beside Doc Zirkin's hencoop."

"How'll we borrow it?"

Spooner scratched his backside. "That," he said, "won't be a problem at all."

"How come?" I asked Spooner.

"Ya see, while I was hid, I heard Doc in the barn, hitching up his mare. Then, and this here is the best part, I heard him say to Mrs. Zirkin that they'd best hurry if they'd ever get their buggy to Setonville by suppertime. Then off they went. Due north at a full-out trot."

I slapped old Spooner on his beefy shoulder. Not too

hard. "Good work, Jitwell. You're a regular Sherlock Holmes."

"And you can be Doctor Watson, his pal."

I stood up. "Spooner, the only doctor I'm concerned with right now is Doc Zirkin."

"Boy, I'm sure glad," said Spooner, getting up on his feet.

"About what?"

"We sure are lucky," said Spooner, "that Doc Zirkin believes in *soaking*."

I giggled. Because for once, dear old Spooner was right. Part of my plan involved a good soaking, and whipping the plan into action on Saturday had a lot to do with the stage-acting ability of Spooner Jitwell.

"Wait up, Hub."

Running, I was at least ten paces ahead of Spooner, who wasn't exactly built for hustling. I was glad Spooner was chubby. Were he a skinny-bean like me, my plan just wouldn't work on Miss Sashay Freshmeadow.

As we pulled up breathless at Doc Zirkin's back stoop, Spooner pointed. "There she is."

And there it was, Doc Zirkin's tub.

"Come on," I told Spooner. "You carry the uphill end, on account that you have more muscles than I do."

"I sure do."

After the first thirty or forty feet, I was sort of surprised how heavy a big copper bathtub could weigh. Somehow we carried it. Or dragged it. Keeping out of sight as best we could, we sneaked the tub through

Aubrey Toonbill's back lot, over a fence, then floated it across Woodson's Crick, and up the riverbank to where Doc Zirkin's copper bathtub would do the most good:

At the home of Miss Sashay Freshmeadow.

Luckily for us, and for our overall plan, Miss Sashay was sitting in a rocking chair on her side porch, fanning herself cool. We set the tub down and waved.

"Smile," I whispered to Spooner.

"Why?"

"Because," I said, "a good salesman always has to smile to make a sale. And don't forget what you're supposed to say."

"I won't," said Spooner.

"Afternoon, boys," said Miss Sashay. She sure was pretty, even though she didn't look like she gave her knife and fork much of a rest at mealtime.

"How do, Miss Freshmeadow," I said, smiling.

"School must be out early," she said.

"Yes'm," I said. "Usual is on Friday."

"What do you boys have there?"

"Just a tub," said Spooner.

"Are you planning to take your Saturday bath a day early?" She got up off the rocker and approached us. "My, it's sizable."

"It's for Spooner," I said. This statement, I had earlier concluded, would be believed by any nose that ever caught a whiff of Spooner Jitwell after a hard run. "We borrowed the tub from Doc Zirkin," I said, "while he's out of town."

"My stars. Must be *heavy*."

"That," I told her, "is sort of Spooner's problem, too. Doc says he's too chubby."

"And," said Spooner, "unless I lose some pounds, nobody'll want to *marry* me."

The expression on Miss Sashay's face told me that we'd made it to first base.

Behind my back I crossed my fingers.

"Is that so?" she said.

"Soaking," said Spooner, "is how fat folks like me get slender."

"A medical fact," I added.

"Mercy me," said Miss Sashay Freshmeadow, her pretty face brightening with sudden interest.

"All I do," said Spooner, "is just sit in this here tub, out in the *sunlight*, and soak in the warm water. Do that, according to Doc, and the pounds practically *fall* off."

"When do you plan to start, Spooner?" I asked him, knowing full well what his answer would be.

"All day Sunday," he said.

"Good idea," I said quickly. "I reckon by Sunday evening you'll be slender as a willow switch."

"And someday," said Spooner, "I'll be lean enough to wed my sweetheart."

"And live happily ever after," I said. As I spoke, I saw Miss Freshmeadow touch the tub. She was one hooked fish.

"Hmm," she mumbled.

"Well," I said, "I guess we best get going, even

though this tub weighs over a ton. Sure wish we didn't have to lug it all the way to Spooner's house."

"Yeah," said Spooner. "Sure is a pity we don't have a place to pasture it."

As I pretended, along with Spooner, to get myself back into a tub-lifting position, I got a good look at Miss Sashay's face. Like she had glass skin, I could almost see the wheels inside her head; and sure enough, she spoke right up.

"Well now, boys, seeing as it's sort of a hot day for bathtub carrying, you could always leave your tub right here with me."

"We could?"

"Why certainly," she said. "Then perhaps tomorrow, after the bicycle race, you might both stop by and pick it up."

"Miss Freshmeadow," I said, "you certainly are a very thoughtful lady. But I suppose the decision is really up to Spooner, seeing as he's the body that can't wait to *soak off the pounds*—as Doc says."

"Unless I do," Spooner spoke up with a big grin, "I don't guess I'll ever be wispy enough to marry my best girl."

"What a gallant thought," Miss Sashay said to Spooner, "and just who, pray tell, might your sweetheart be?"

Spooner smiled. "Amoeba May Kiliper."

"Pull," I whispered in the dark.

Spooner yanked the length of fishing line that we had just buried under the leaves and brush along the road-side. No sooner had he tugged on the line then up popped a tip-up, looking exactly like one of the red flags that already marked the race course.

"Does it work, Hub?"

"Like a charm. And the fish we're going to catch is one named Mr. Montana Muldoon."

The time must have been close to midnight. An hour earlier, Spooner and I had sneaked out of our houses; so here we were, preparing by moonlight.

"Tomorrow's the big day, Hub."

"Right," I said, "and keep your voice down. We don't want to get caught."

"Are you sure you saw what you climbed up the tree to see this afternoon?" Spooner asked.

"I saw it."

"You sure it'll work?"

"It's got to," I said. "Otto Piddle told me how Montana Muldoon forces other bicycles off the road. Otto says Muldoon is a bully, whether he's on a bicycle or off."

"We'll fix him," said Spooner. "Are you sure Miss Sashay Freshmeadow won't be watching the bike race, instead of taking a bath in the sunshine?"

"Yup," I said.

"How can you be so sure, Hub?"

"Logic," I said. "Now if Otto was riding *his* bicycle in the race, she'd be watching every lap, and praying for Otto like he was butterscotch."

"But he can't. He's injured."

"Yup," I whispered. "Now then, next we use our shovel under these bushes."

"Okay," said Spooner.

Spooner did the digging, making sure at least three of the thick green shrubs behind Miss Freshmeadow's secluded backyard were close to being uprooted. Around each bush I tied lengths of clothesline that we'd borrowed, with the help of Spooner's jackknife, from Elva Watson's washline.

"The angle's got to be right," said Spooner.

"It is. That's why I climbed up in that tree, so I could see the turn in the road, plan where our tip-ups go, and slow down Mr. Montana Muldoon to an absolute whoa."

"Hub, if this plan of yours works, I'm going to vote for you to be President of the whole darn United States."

"Thanks," I said. "Here's how I figure the race'll go."

"How?"

"Well, I saw Miss Guppy practice on one of Otto's race bicycles."

"So what?"

"According to my eye, she's not the fastest cyclist in town."

"How fast is she?"

"Spooner, I was right surprised. She may not be able to outpedal Montana Muldoon, but my guess is she's a mite faster than either Ernie or Whit. But only for the first lap. After that, her legs might tire a bit."

"I want Miss Guppy to win, Hub."

"You do?"

"Yup."

"Seems to me you were saying that you didn't like school, and you didn't cotton to Miss Guppy, and you were planning to quit."

"I don't plan to quit," said Spooner.

"You don't, eh?"

"No, beeause planning a bicycle race is a whole lot more fun than a dumb old plan to quit school."

"Now you're talking." Inside, I felt right pleased about Spooner Jitwell's reborn determination.

"Thanks," he said.

"But what I really want you to do, Spooner, is dig."

"Hub . . ."

"Yeah?"

"How come I have to do all the digging and all *you* do is the overall plan?"

"Because you're stronger at digging, and I'm foxier at plans."

Spooner sighed. Spitting on his hands, he continued to dig around the three bushes, while I paced off the distance to our next tip-up, our fake red flag.

The clock in the Town Hall tower struck once. One lonely *bong*.

"I'm near done," said Spooner. "And done in."

"Are you certain you dug deep enough?"

"Yup."

"Remember now, Spooner, these three bushes have to be looser than a bad tooth. Without this gate we're making, Miss Freshmeadow's backyard is more private than a meat locker."

"Maybe we ought to test 'em, Hub."

"Good idea. I think your brain is starting to work on target."

"Honest?"

"I mean it, Spooner. Ya see, all you gotta do is *try*."

"But I'm dumb so doggone often."

"Now get this straight, Spooner." My finger pointed at his head. "You're not dumb. But I think I know your trouble."

"What is it?"

"Shh," I warned. "Let's not wake up all of Chump's Landing."

"Okay," whispered Spooner. "Now *tell* me, Hub. What's my trouble?"

"You're lazy. You don't apply yourself."

"Nuts to you, Hubert. All you do is measure and pace off, while I work the shovel. You're all dry and I'm a wash of sweat." Spooner threw down his spade.

"Easy, old pal. What I'm aiming to tell you is, if you dig into your geography book like you dig under bushes, you might savvy the difference between Alaska and Delaware."

"Hmm," snorted Spooner. "Maybe you're right."

"Come on," I said.

"Where to?"

"Goose Gifford's place."

"What'll we do there?"

"Doggone you, Spooner. I already *told* you the plan. That's the trouble with you, and Miss Guppy told you the same thing."

"Like what?"

"You don't *listen*. Best you tie a gag over your mouth, pull the corks out of your ears, and pay a little mind as to what folks are saying. Especially people like Miss Guppy, who just happens to know a thing or two."

We walked along carrying a shovel, a fishline, and a roll of tape, plus an armload of tip-ups.

"Hub . . ."

"Now what?"

"I don't guess Miss Guppy likes me much."

"Hogwash. She sure does."

"Maybe *she* does a little. But I don't guess Odessa likes me at all."

"Maybe she could."

"If I soak off some weight? Or wash?"

"Right. Just maybe Odessa Langford figures that a guy too lazy for soap is also too lazy to kiss."

Spooner smiled, and the moonlight down through the tree leaves danced on his wide grin. "Hub, I don't guess I'd ever be too lazy to kiss Odessa Langford. But all she thinks about is baseball."

"Don't be too sure," I told Spooner.

Arriving at Goose Gifford's, we accomplished what we'd come to do, which was to loosen the latch that penned in his flock of white geese. And then tie a length of line to the latch peg. The latch was stuck. When it came loose, Spooner banged the gate, creating a loud crack of wood against wood.

A dog barked.

And worse, every sleeping goose woke up and started honking like it was near Christmas in a hungry town. The sudden noise made me wet all over, fear of capture oozing from my every pore. Goose Gifford owned a shotgun.

"Run," I whispered.

Needlessly, as old Spooner had already taken to his heels. We didn't stop until we'd splashed across Woodson's Crick and were close to home, his and mine.

"See ya tomorrow, Spooner."

"Okay. Good night, Hub."

I said, "Don't let the squirrels getcha."

"We're both nuts," he said. "But ain't it fun? Ya know, maybe for the big day tomorrow, I'll celebrate with some soap and water. And a clean shirt."

"Now you're planning."

"Hub, I never told ya, but Odessa Langford said that I sort of smelled worse than Harv Putnam's sow."

"No you don't, Spooner. You don't smell at all like Alice."

"What do I smell like?"

"Eunice."

"Good luck," we told Miss Guppy.

"Thank you, boys." With an arm around each of our necks, Miss Guppy presented a quick hug to Spooner and me, kissing each of us a peck on the cheek. "That'll bring me home."

We watched her push her bicycle through the rapidly gathering crowd in the direction of the starting line. She wore a bright red shirt, a man's overalls, work shoes, and a red baseball cap. Two ladies pointed at her and snickered to each other, as if they thought they were better than she was. Well, they weren't, because nobody in the whole town of Chump's Landing was any nicer than Miss Guppenfeffer.

"Our teacher," I said. It made me proud to say it.

Suddenly the crowd mumbled.

Following the noise, Spooner and I trotted around the corner by Rickert's Grocery to see what was going on. I sure didn't like what I saw, the challenger from Setonville. Spooner almost whispered the man's name.

"Montana Muldoon."

Mr. Muldoon was wearing a black undershirt, cut low in a loop in front to expose his hairy chest, although he was baldheaded. Below his big red nose, there was his mighty black mustache, like the horns of a mean bull. His black trousers were cut off real high. Muldoon had the legs of a plowhorse.

"Lifting weights, Hub," said Spooner. "That's how he grew all them muscles."

"*Those* muscles."

Spooner smiled at me. "Yeah, *those*."

Hardly anyone seemed to be watching Ernie Kapp, Whitney Mitford, Miss Guppy, or any of the other cyclists. Nine in all, I counted. The eyes of Chump's Landing seemed to focus on none other than the muscular man in black, Mr. Montana Muldoon.

"Even his bike is black, Hub."

"And his soul, most likely."

Not everyone in our village had come to Main Street to witness the start of the Chump's Landing Overland Obstacle Bicycle Race. Year after year, lots of folks stayed home, to sit in the shade of their porches to watch the riders pedal by, seeing as the race course wandered all around the outskirts of the town. A few kids were up in trees.

Music flared up.

"It's the band, Hub. Let's go hear."

As there was still plenty of time before Mayor Smather would fire his pistol into the air to start the race, Spooner and I edged through citizens toward the music. And there stood the Chump's Landing Marching Musical Marvels in their bright lavender and silver uniforms, performing their worst upon John Philip Sousa. Yet they were the best the town had to offer, and no one seemed to care whether or not the trombone and cornet lagged a few notes behind.

Mr. Rickert tooted the cornet. Mr. Quimby, the slide trombone. Mr. Kiliper, proud sire of Amoeba May, fingered a fluent clarinet, standing next to the reed section's other two members: Amos Goover on the tenor saxophone, and Abe Polaski with his huge contrabassoon. The youngest member, standing somewhere inside his oversized uniform, was a kid I knew at school, Albin Hucker, who could ting a triangle. All in all, they produced a noise that would almost rot your socks.

"Look at Otis," said Spooner.

Otis Dorf, our local blacksmith, was the town's largest citizen; and he also played the band's tiniest instrument, the fife. Next to Otis stood a grinning Goose Gifford, who, though in uniform, did not play anything at all. It was Goose, however, who carried the enormous bass drum, thumped with dedicated precision by Philo Mc-

Murtree. A large and lavendar C could be read within the bass drum's booming circle. The drum, because of it's impressive size and weight, was tightly strapped to Goose Gifford's back.

The march that they were now attempting, a cross between "El Capitan" and "Washington Post" mercifully blared to a graduated ending, the leaders waiting patiently for the laggards to honk the final note. One member of the band produced no music whatsoever.

"Hey," said Mr. Rickert, "how come you brought only one cymbal?" to Vint Bozarth.

"Other one's amiss. Couldn't find the doggone thing. I never realized it."

"Realized what?"

Vint said, "I don't guess I ever knew that it's harder to play one cymbal than to play two."

Spooner and I watched Montana Muldoon. As he did his kneebends to loosen up his legs, the muscles of his thighs swelled up bigger than prime beef. Flexing his arms, he winked at several of the ladies as they passed by or stopped to stare at him in rapt disbelief.

I overheard Mayor Smather talking to one of the other officials, all of whom wore orange ribbons to distinguish them from being merely spectators.

"Five laps," said the mayor. "Around the town is a two miler, so that makes—let's see now, he counted on his fingers—*ten* miles in all. Uphill, downhill, across Woodson's Crick twice each lap, not to forget the hurdle south of the livery stable, and the other one—"

"Otto," I hollered and waved.

Looking our way, Otto smiled and waved back. "Hi there, boys."

Otto Piddle was walking with a cane, but the sling

was no longer hugging his arm. I was real happy to see that he had been invited to wear the orange ribbon of a referee.

"Next year, Otto," I said.

"Sure hope so."

"Yeah," said Spooner. "You'll be right out front on the last lap, right where you belong."

"Who's going to win?" Otto asked us.

"Miss Guppy," we both answered. "We hope."

"That'd be a caution," he said, smiling. "An excellent lady, Hossanah Guppenfeffer, and I wish her all the luck. But then, old Ernie and Whit are good old boys. Maybe they'll whip up the ponies and finish respectable. Neither one is getting any younger."

"What about Muldoon?" I asked.

As we talked, the three of us watched Mr. Montana Muldoon oiling the sprocket of the big wheel of his black bicycle. Then the little wheel in back. His oilcan sounded meaner than a morning mule. *Konk, keekonk, keekonk.*

"Muldoon's an ornery cuss," said Otto. "Tell your teacher best not to crowd him around the curves. If you hug the rail, Muldoon can do fearful things to bike spokes. He files notches in his pedals that cut metal, or flesh."

"We'll tell her," I said. "But I bet she already knows. Miss Guppy knows a whole lot."

"Sure does. Say, would you boys like to view the trophy?"

"You bet."

Walking slowly with Otto, we climbed the three steps up onto the front stoop of Quimby's Drygoods Store, closed for the occasion. There it sat, a silvery masterpiece, a tiny rider astride a leaning bicycle; agleam, even in the shade. The trophy was being guarded, as it sat on a table, between two local ladies who sported orange ribbons, Mrs. Olga Hallerby and Miss Wilma Finch.

"A real beauty, Hub," said Spooner, shaking his head a single shake of devout admiration. As he spoke, I pictured our coveted silver trophy in the hairy arms of Montana Muldoon, and shuddered. Would he get to keep it for a whole year?

"See ya later, guys," said Otto.

"We'll be around," said Spooner.

"And don't," warned Otto, "get yourselves into too much mischief."

Spooner and I poked around through the swelling congregation until we spotted Amoeba May Kiliper, with her mother.

"Howdy do, Horrace," said Amoeba May. As her ma turned to speak to another lady, Amoeba May Kiliper blew me a kiss, an act which good old Spooner Jitwell happened to notice.

Spooner, in his high-pitched girlie voice that he used to twit me, said, "Howdy do, Horrace," and blew another kiss my way. Well, I guess I'd just let the matter pass me by; seeing as old Spooner was too husky to scrap with and too much fun to hate. He would have kept it up all day, but right then something else happened to nudge his mind, and mine, off the subject of kissing.

"It's gone," said Doc Zirkin.

Spooner Jitwell and I sort of looked at each other as we both took a few steps backward, in order to hide behind the band.

"What's gone, Doc?" someone asked.

"My tub got stolen. Yessir, some rotten crook sneaked over in the night and lifted it. And I *know* who did it."

"Who?"

"Soon as I locate Sheriff Spinelli, I intend to bring the law down on the head of that rascal. And stick him right where he belongs. Behind bars."

I was starting to sweat and too scared to run. From the sound of Doc Zirkin's voice, I could tell that he was too sore to be cured by either soaking or massage. Shouting, and waving his hands, Doc Zirkin seemed to be in one heck of a rampage.

"Who's the thief, Doc?"

"Doc Kink."

"Go!" yelled Mayor Smather.

As he discharged his pistol into the air, all we heard was an empty click. But the fact that our mayor had somehow forgotten to load his gun had little effect on the start of the Chump's Landing Overland Obstacle Race.

All nine riders, held on high at either side by two assistants, pumped forward and the race was on. Nine pairs of goggles leaned forward, staring straight ahead at the first turn, as nine pairs of feet worked a like number of pedals.

"Come back," shouted Mayor Smather, "because it's just not an official start unless I . . ."

But no rider stopped. As hats were thrown into the air from the heads of spirited onlookers, citizens shouted, and half the band played "Stars and Stripes Forever," the other musicians seeming to be equally partial to "Nola."

"There they go, Hub."

"Come on," I said to Spooner.

"Where to?"

"Please don't ask so many questions," I said. "All we have to do now is follow our overall plan."

Jumping up on a rainbarrel, Spooner and I managed to climb up on the roof of the livery stable, where we could have ourselves a long view of the first lap. Clusters of people were yelling away down the road, helping us to pinpoint the precise position of the racers.

"Who's ahead, Hub?"

As I extended my arm to point, a black blob pumped through a clearing in the trees, pulling away from the eight other bicycles that followed.

"Montana Muldoon," I sighed.

"Where's Miss Guppy?"

"Dead last."

"Are ya sure, Hub?"

"There!" I pointed quickly at the eight racers that bunched in for the far turn. A red shirt was riding in the rear, eating dust. Yet she wasn't going to quit.

"Come on, Miss Guppy," yelled Spooner.

I sort of prayed to myself. Work those pedals, Miss Guppy, and don't let Montana Muldoon get too far ahead of you.

"Let's go, Hub."

"Go where?"

"Best we do something. And fast."

The gray splinters of the stable roof pricked my hands as Spooner and I slid down to safety. Cutting behind the feedstore and through a fence, we arrived at the roadside, hiding low in the tall blue-daisy weeds behind Ed Fellbright's corn crib.

"Here they come, Hub."

Spooner was right. Around the bend in the dusty road, we saw Mr. Montana Muldoon leaning into the turn, splashing through the mud puddle and coming our way. Behind him, pedaling almost as fast, rode the eight others. As we waited, I saw Miss Guppy; in ninth place, but still keeping up.

"Muldoon's going to win, Hub."

"Easy," I mumbled to Spooner. "The first lap isn't even halfway over. And when it is, there are four more laps to go."

"How soon'll we try our tricks?"

"Well," I said, "soon as Montana Muldoon gets way ahead, as he's bound to do."

After all nine bicycles whizzed by us in a colorful blur, Spooner and I scrambled back toward the center of town. Folks were cheering and hollering, urging the local contestants to pedal harder to catch up. But the bike that raced through town for the first lap, well ahead, was the black bicycle of Montana Muldoon.

"What'll we do, Hub?"

Reaching into my pocket, I withdrew my map, unfolding it carefully so the worn creases wouldn't rip. Spooner had been correct. My map was closer to looking more like a smudgy mess than an overall plan. It resembled an after-supper napkin.

"Now," I said. "Now we strike."

"Where?"

"Goose Gifford's geese."

We ran. People were everywhere along the roadside, cheering and rooting for their favorite bicycles and riders. Dodging through the crowd slowed us up a bit, but Spooner and I made it to where we wanted to go. The closer we got, the more my nose told me that we were in the vicinity of a flock of geese. Inside a pen.

"Where's the fishing line, Hub?"

"I can't find it."

"You were the one who hid it."

"I know," I told Spooner. "But it was dark last night. Objects sort of look different in the daylight."

Beating around the bushes, we looked for our first glimpse of a fishline, the other end of which was secretly knotted around a peg that held the latch of the goose pen. In the distance, I could hear folks shouting; so I knew at least one bike had rounded the turn and come into view.

"Ouch," said Spooner.

Turning around, I saw Spooner Jitwell lying on the ground, facedown. But stretched across his foot was a stretched-out fishing line. Looking up, I noticed the gate was opening. Our overall plan was commencing to work.

Out of the wooden gate charged Goose Gifford's prize flock of white geese, exactly as I had hoped. Honking, flapping, smothering the road just as Montana Muldoon bore down on at least a score of our feathery friends.

"*Yaaahhhhh!*" yelled Muldoon.

Wagons have brakes. Bicycles don't. And geese are far too fast and too smart to get themselves run over. But I figured that Montana Muldoon wouldn't know that. And he didn't. Instead of riding forward, he twisted the handlebars to the right, thrashing into Miss Amelia Matchett's rose bushes, thorns and all. Spooner and I had learned, from earlier experiences, that Miss Matchett was somebody to avoid. Out she came, armed with a sweeping broom, which she used to convince Mr. Muldoon that he and her rose bushes were never again to be united. Not even by accident. Her broom seemed to have a temper all its own.

Before he could mount his bicycle, the eight other riders pedaled by, even though the air was full of goose honks and a flurry of white feathers. Geese flapped everywhere. One excited gander darted through the open screen door and into Miss Matchett's parlor. This, it appeared, enraged her even more; inspiring her to chase Mr. Muldoon down the road, swiping at him with her broom. Luckily for him, she finally tripped over a goose.

"Hey," said Spooner, "I just noticed, Hub."

"Noticed what?"

"The last bike that went by."

"What about it?"

Spooner smiled. "The rider in last place was *not* wearing a red shirt."

"Hot spit," I said. "That means Miss Guppy passed somebody."

Spotting a ladder leaning against Mrs. Trudeau's cowshed, Spooner and I hurried up the rungs to the peak of the roof. Hanging on to the shaft of a rusty weathervane, I felt the breeze of a hot day in Chump's Landing tickle my face. Trees grew all over town, masking our view of the race. Mostly we saw green leaves; and white geese, honking just about everywhere.

"Look yonder, Hub."

"Where?"

As Spooner pointed, I squinted in the sunshine. Sure enough, I saw three bike riders about to cross Woodson's

Crick. It was Ernie Kapp and Whit Mitford, plus a third bike rider. Halfway across, one bicycle zigged when another zagged; and then all three of them seemed to get tangled up in their underwear. Down they splashed, into shallow water and deep trouble. Soaking wet, each of the trio seemed to be blaming the other two, as the six other bicycles rolled through.

Miss Guppy was in front, but in second place was Montana Muldoon, and gaining. Pumping up the bank, he passed her.

"Step two, Hub?"

"Right," I said.

Running through Amos Goover's barn and out the far side, Spooner and I pulled up breathless at the spot where we'd hidden a length of clothesline, the former lanyard that had once so proudly waved Elva Watson's underwear.

"Neck high," I told Spooner.

Stretching it across the road was what we'd accomplished last night. Buried in the dust, the rope didn't show. Spooner positioned himself across the roadway from where I was hiding. His hands were ready on the clothesline, as were mine.

"Now?"

"No," I tried to tell him. "Not until Muldoon is ready to ride by. Here he comes."

Patience, I then decided as I saw him pull the rope, was what Spooner Jitwell ought to work on. Sure enough, the rope whipped up too early; but Muldoon's quick eye ducked his head. As I read the frown of disappointment on Spooner's face, I saw him ease his rope. But he failed to slacken it enough. The rope snared the front of Miss Guppy's bike, jerking Spooner out of the bushes like a hooked sunfish.

"Let's go!" I yelled to Spooner.

Luckily for old Spooner, he let loose of the rope, because Miss Guppy never even slowed down. Her bike was pumping at full throttle. She sure had worked up a full head of steam.

And yet Montana Muldoon was winning.

-14-

"Last lap," I told Spooner.

"Best we hurry, Hub, or Miss Guppy won't have a chance for the silver trophy."

We hustled.

Thank the good golly, I was thinking as we scrambled through the thick bushes behind Miss Sashay Freshmeadow's house, that Doc Zirkin didn't yet know the location of his tub. Thank goodness it was a sunny day. And I was even more thankful that a certain pretty (but chubby) lady had decided to heed the sermon that Spooner and I had so carefully preached. About soaking off the pounds.

"Wow! There she is, Hub."

Spooner smiled. Sure enough, there was Miss Sashay Freshmeadow in the tub, in total privacy and in the sunshine; but *not* in her clothes. Spooner's eyes were wider than usual.

"Ya know, Hub, I don't guess I ever seen—"

"Ever *saw*."

"Okay, ever saw. How in the heck, Hub can you think about proper English when you're watching a gal take a bath?"

To be perfectly honest, I wasn't really thinking much about grammar. What I really thought about was Amoeba May Kiliper. And kissing. But then I forced my attention to a more pressing matter, a man by the name of Mr. Montana Muldoon.

"Spooner," I said, "let's hasten."

But old Spooner wasn't hearing me, because he was still staring at the copper bathtub; and even harder at its occupant, who wasn't quite covered with bubbles from Doc Zirkin's soapy elixir. There sure was a lot of Miss Freshmeadow to cover.

"Come on, Spooner. Locate the ropes to loosen the bushes. I'll work the tip-up flags to reroute the race."

As I spoke, a cyclist whizzed by. But he wasn't the leader. It was Whit, still on his fourth lap. With the rope in my hand, I watched the bend in the road, waiting for a black bicycle ridden by Montana Muldoon.

"Here he comes," I said. "Now!"

Spooner didn't budge, as I guess a sudden breeze had blown off bits of lather. Spooner just stared, and grinned.

"Pull!" I yelled at Spooner.

As I hollered, I yanked my line, lifting up a pair of

tip-ups to slightly alter the race course. Then I presented Spooner with a sudden kick, which jolted his thoughts away from bathtubs and more in the direction of moving a bush or two.

"Now?" asked Spooner.

"Yes, *now*. Pull, ya big lunkhead. Harder. Here comes Muldoon!"

It worked. We pulled. The bushes parted, and into the private backyard of Miss Sashay Freshmeadow rode Mr. Montana Muldoon. Earlier I had noticed how wide Spooner Jitwell's eyes had popped. But certainly not as wide as the eyes of Mr. Muldoon. Perhaps it was an error on her part, but that happened to be the very moment that Miss Freshmeadow sort of stood up. And right then I noticed something. Strange thing about Doc Zirkin's elixir bubbles—they really don't cling to a bather or offer too much concealment. Miss Freshmeadow sure got Mr. Muldoon's undivided attention.

"Oh!" said Miss Freshmeadow.

"Ah," said Mr. Muldoon.

Such was his surprise that his eyes kept staring, his legs kept pedaling; his bicycle sideswiped an elm, bounced off a willow, and then headed for the big copper bathtub.

Crash!

Just as Miss Freshmeadow jumped out of the tub, Mr. Muldoon dived in, right over the handlebars. Miss Sashay reached for her pink bathtowel, one corner of which was pinned beneath the big black bicycle.

"Hey!"

Someone yelled, so Spooner and I turned around to look. We saw Doc Zirkin about the same time as he saw Montana Muldoon in his bathtub.

"Thief!" yelled Doc.

Miss Freshmeadow tried to crawl underneath her towel. Sudsy bubbles wafted into the sky, along with the fragrance of Doc Zirkin's chiropractic elixir. Not to mention the colorful language that Doc was using, which made Miss Freshmeadow cover her ears. Good thing, for not much else was covered.

"You stole my soaking tub," hollered Doc Zirkin, pointing at Muldoon. "You and your fat girl friend."

"*Fat?*" Miss Sashay Freshmeadow's face suddenly turned much pinker than the rest of her. Pinker even than her towel, which Doc was standing on. Muldoon's bicycle lay on its side, its big front wheel spinning around and around, as though it wondered when this nightmare would stop.

"You heard me," said Doc. "I said *fat*."

I was amazed to see Miss Sashay Freshmeadow push Doc Zirkin backward, causing him to trip and fall into his own tub, just as Mr. Muldoon was trying to get out. Now both men tried to climb up from inside the tub. Seeing as Muldoon was already splashing around inside, there wasn't much room left for Doc.

"Look out," hollered Spooner.

I jumped out of the way in time, as five bicycles came bumping into the yard. The bike in front was ridden by someone in a bright red shirt, Miss Guppy. She was in the lead.

"Go, Miss Guppy, *go!*" I yelled.

She just missed the tub, but the other cyclists did not fare as well. Ernie Kapp's front wheel nipped the edge of the tub, and out tumbled Doc, just as Ernie landed on Muldoon. His eyes rolled sleepily as his head sunk slowly into a hill of billowing bubbles.

A whistle blew. Turning, I saw Sheriff Spinelli arrive. "What's going on here?" He pointed at Miss Freshmeadow. "You're under arrest—for indecent exposure."

"No," yelled Doc.

"Help," blubbered Montana Muldoon.

"Not *her*," said a wet and soppy Doc Zirkin, who pointed at Muldoon. "He's the one who stole it."

Sheriff Spinelli pulled out his notebook. "Maybe I best take down all the facts. Okay, now *who* stole this here bicycle?"

"That's not what was stolen," hollered Doc.

"Well then," said Sheriff Spinelli, "then let's find out the crook that stole this towel. I'll need it for evidence."

Miss Freshmeadow shrieked.

Suddenly, it happened. No one could see anything or anyone, because Miss Freshmeadow's backyard filled quickly with the entire flock of escaped geese. The air was a blizzard of white feathers, and then I saw the cause of their hysteria. Behind them, his hands holding a net on a pole while his back still carried the enormous bass drum, ran Goose Gifford.

"Come back, Goose," said Philo McMurtree, chasing the drum with his "potato masher," which was how he referred to his singular drumstick. "Come back. We haven't finished 'Nola.'"

Geese honked an ear-splitting babble, running or flapping in every direction. One goose caught its leg inside the bell of Mr. Quimby's slide trombone. Mr. Quimby blew it out, but the note didn't sound much like "Nola."

I tried to say something to Spooner, to suggest that we leave the scene before getting arrested by Sheriff Spinelli,

but I couldn't talk. Too many goose feathers in my mouth.

"Look quick, Hub."

I looked. Montana Muldoon was back up on his bicycle, and his powerful legs began to churn forward. Then I saw something worse. Somehow, in the blizzard of goose feathers, Miss Guppy had gotten herself turned around and was heading back toward the tub. That was when Mayor Smather arrived and fired his pistol into the air.

"There," said the mayor. "Now we got an official start, because you see, unless I—"

A goose fell to the ground.

"You shot one of my prize geese!" wailed Goose Gifford. "Sheriff, arrest this man."

Goose Gifford whirled to face the only law officer in town; and as he did so, the giant drum spun with him,

banging Muldoon harder than a bat ever hit a baseball. Down went Montana Muldoon, his ankle entangled in the loop of a slide trombone, which was still being tooted and slid by Mr. Quimby.

And so Mr. Muldoon was arrested for stealing a bathtub, for being a peeping tom, for indirectly shooting a goose, and for the wanton destruction of a trombone.

So that's how Montana Muldoon did *not* win the silver trophy for the Chump's Landing Overland Obstacle Bicycle Race. No, he didn't win.

Miss Guppy did, because our teacher was practically the only soul in town that wasn't either soaking wet, arrested, or bitten by a goose.

Photo by Nancy Hoffman

Robert Newton Peck
and his son Christopher Haven Peck

ROBERT NEWTON PECK comes from a long line of Vermont farmers. His books include *A Day No Pigs Would Die, Millie's Boy, Path of Hunters, Eagle Fur, Patooie, Soup, King of Kazoo, Soup and Me* (now on ABC TV network) and the recently published *Soup for President*. His historical trilogy on Fort Ticonderoga is *Fawn, Hang for Treason* and *The King's Iron*. In addition to his writing and lecturing, Robert Newton Peck is the director of the Rollins College Writers Conference. He lives with his wife and two children in Longwood, Florida.